LONG TIM

A JOURNEY THROUGH EYES OF THE BLIND

TANMAI JAIN

Made with ♥ on the Notion Press Platform
www.notionpress.com

Contents

Preface   *v*

1. Human Brain Or The Bat's Instinct!   1

2. Be Curious To Know Us   6

3. How The Blind Reads   11

4. Our Race Against Time   16

5. The Mental And Emotional Conflicts   21

6. Controversially Navigating The World   26

7. The White Cane   31

8. Our Challenges   36

9. Why Do We Hide   41

10. Me, Myself And Mostly Others   46

11. Making Choices   51

12. Relearning How To Live Life   55

13. The Guilt Challenge   59

14. Smart Tech Makes Blind Smarter   63

Preface

On a stormy evening when the lights went out and my eyes could not adjust to the darkness for a while, I couldn't have known that's how life was going to treat me almost forever.

I am Tanmai, whomever - or whatever - that is. Despite my belief that I think I know who I am, I admit to periodic doubt.

One thing of which I am certain however, is I am not a category. Many entangled characteristics and qualities make me "Me." On the simplest level, I am human, gender: male.

A product of nature, a creation of circumstances.

I am: Tanmai, NOT a category.

I'm a thinking, sensible soul. In my mind, I can articulate important theories and once in a while, when I'm very fortunate, even inspire others.

I have philosophies, beliefs and values. With those as signboards, I have developed a roadmap that I presume will take me to wherever my final destination is.

From time to time, I hesitate and fall, but I'm learning and growing. Therefore, I must be determined and sometimes absolute stubborn.

I am also confused and wise, excited and bored, happy and sad, loving and lost, frightened
and brave, leader and follower, almost always hopeful.

When family or friends meet me, we hug, the warmth of his or her body held close to mine in a loving embrace;

"Hi Tanmai, how are you?"

It is my name, not a category, spoken affectionately by someone about whom I
deeply care. They do not call to me by what shows on the health scale or on a section of any disability certificate.

I am not described as physically challenged.

My value, who I am, what I do, my legacy, does not fluctuate with the number of obstacles reflected by my karma, nor by how many miles I have walked dreadfully.

That one category, although a description of a single, observable, component of WHAT I am, is virtually insignificant in the long run of WHO I am and what I am capable of
achieving.

I am far more unbelievable than what any category, anywhere could ever make known!

I learnt about living with a partially distorted vision. Following sounds and relying on touching objects, I had a unique experience.

You must be getting curious to know more about how do people with visual impairment live their lives and what do their surroundings mean to them.

This book is a result of that pursuit for understanding and will go a long way in helping you become more comfortable in interacting with people who have visual impairment.

As you allow this understanding to settle, just remember that blindness is not a defect or a stigma. It is a characteristic, just as sight is,

And Helen Keller's words capture this fact beautifully:

"I can see, and that is why I can be happy, in what you call the dark, but which to me is golden.
I can see a God-made world, not a manmade world."

CHAPTER ONE

HUMAN BRAIN OR THE BAT'S INSTINCT!

Low vision talks about a visual loss that cannot be improved by surgery or glasses.

There are many types of low vision, and it is not simply a variation between fully sighted or completely blind.

Low vision can be visible in a variety of ways, such as difficulty with reading, trouble telling apart colors and having reduced outer or central vision. It also affects a person's ability to perform daily activities like reading, writing, cooking or driving.

But as they say, the brain has the ability to compensate for the loss.

I lost my vision when I was 16, triggering all my other senses to recover from the damage.

Very early in life, I started using all my healthy senses to remember things well. But, I pay attention to sounds more because I don't always have a sixth sense.

When one looses their vision, the brain starts relying more on the other senses to make sense of the world around. This upgraded attention can improve the remaining senses, like hearing and touch, which may have been neglected before.

Blind people have better audio processing skills, as we rely more heavily on these senses for information. We also have better navigation abilities and spatial memory, as we rely on mental maps to navigate our environment.

With time and practice, our brain learns to depend on these senses more, and they become more trustworthy. This helps to compensate for our loss of vision.

Additionally, few blind people use a method called "echo-location" to find out where things are. We make sounds by clicking our tongue, snapping our fingers, or tapping a cane. The sound bounces off objects and comes back to us, telling us where things are and how big they are. Using tongue clicks is the best way to get a good sense of space around us because the mouth and ears work together naturally.

Some of us don't like making clicking sounds at first as we're afraid of drawing attention to ourselves. And since we can't see who's staring at us , we naturally imagine the worst.

Well, isn't it funny how our minds work?

Even sighted people are always imagining the worst-case scenario. And when it comes to blind people, it's even worse! Since we can't see who's staring at us, we're probably imagining some enemy only.

I mean, who knows what could be hiding in the darkness?

It could be a friendly face, or it could be an enemy ready to attack.

I use my good hearing and some basic math to figure out how far away things are based on how long it takes for sound to reach me.

So I mostly navigate using my sense of hearing, or by listening for traffic noise, or other auditory cues to help me orient myself and move through my environment.

Therefore, we often rely heavily on our sense of hearing to navigate the world around us, identify possible risks, and to communicate with others.

Audio signals can provide a wealth of information for us. For example, the sound of traffic can help decide when it is safe for us to cross the road, while the sound of footsteps can alert us to the presence of a person nearby. The sound of a train station or a fountain outside a mall , can help us take note of nearby landmarks.

This skill is crucial for us to live independently, as it allows us to sense potential dangers and make informed decisions. By using auditory cues, we can locate objects, understand layout of a place and communicate with others. Without this ability, we would face significant barriers in living a safe life.

Overall, the ability to observe and understand audio clues is essential for us to live freely.

Just like anyone else, we sometimes need help to learn new things or get used to a new place. But, we still like to live independently.

Some blind people use echoes to get information, but only a few of us make sounds to hear the echoes. Some are better at this than others, and just being blind doesn't mean we're good at it naturally. However, with a lot of practice and feedback from others, we can get better at it.

Numerous attempts have already shown that even blindfolded

people without visual impairment can learn to detect objects in their surroundings after just a short period of time.

Most people rely on their sight to understand their surroundings and as muman beings evolved, hearing became less important for finding the way because it can be misleading. However, it's completely different when it comes to blind people trying to navigate. Some of us would use sound to navigate and do it very well. While others may still use a cane to find doorways.

If you meet someone who is visually impaired, it's important to remember that we are just like everyone else. We may have some vision, even if it's not perfect, and we don't want to be treated differently. We are just like you, except we can't see what we want to see. We don't want to be pampered or treated with pity, we just want to be treated like regular people, witty and gritty.

You don't need to avoid using words like "look" or "see" around us because we won't be offended.

It's just more important to respect our individuality and ensuring our dignity and full inclusion in society. Remember, our senses of touch, sound, and smell compensate for our lack of vision.

My sense of touch can detect textures better than any fashion designer, my sense of hearing can hear a pin drop from a mile away and my sense of smell can tell apart different fragrances in a crowded elevator.

I may not have eyes, but my other senses are like a superhero!

Respecting the independence of blind people means recognizing our capabilities and strengths, and not just focusing on our limitations.

We can excel in fields like literature, music and other creative arts. We can be teachers, public speakers and even successful entrepreneurs. After all, being blind does not necessarily mean that we are unable to live a full and independent life. With the right support and resources, we can overcome many of the challenges we face and succeed in our daily lives.

By giving us the chance to do things for ourselves, you acknowledge our abilities and skills, which helps to build our confidence and self-esteem. Not underestimating our capabilities and Treating us with equality, can make a huge difference. We can make valuable contributions to society in many incredible ways.

CHAPTER TWO

BE CURIOUS TO KNOW US

Charitable assistance is something that may make us feel very small. For example, taking us to our destination or helping us cross the road specially when we have just asked for directions. Or buying grocery for us and or counting money on our behalf. Even picking up something we might have dropped are all judged as overcompensating kindness, which many blind people express as offensive. After all, we have to live our lives on our own everyday and you can't be around all the time.

Take my advice- Do not try to over-help blind people. Why?

Because we're perfectly capable of living our lives just like everyone else. We may need a little bit of extra assistance here and there, but ultimately we are self-sufficient and don't need constant supervision.

I mean, have you ever tried to help a blind person cross the road? It can be quite an adventure. We'll be like, "I'm ok, I'll manage" and then proceed to walk right into a pillar or a wall. But you know what? That's okay. We'll still laugh it off and keep on banging.

When we get on a bus or metro, climb stairs, or walk through crowded places, it can be helpful if someone offers to guide us. Although, it's important for you to ask us first and not force your help on us. If we say we don't need help, you must respect that because your over-care can undermine our self-confidence and create unnecessary dependence on you.

But if we accept, ask how you can best help and follow our lead.

If we ask you for directions, use words like "straight ahead," "turn right," "on your left". DON'T point and say, "It's over there" or "Go that way".

Yes, verbal cues are important when communicating with blind people. Since we cannot see hand movements or facial expressions, we depend heavily on audio information. Therefore, it is very important to use clear and descriptive language to communicate directions, surroundings and ambiances.

Use expressive, imaginative and vibrant language to convey information about the environment, objects or people around us.

If you're unsure of how to communicate effectively with someone who is blind, it's okay to ask us how we prefer to be addressed or to ask for guidance on how to best communicate with us.

Furthermore, spoken signals also provide us with important information about the conversation, including tone, voice modulation and intimations.

Your extra effort in explaining the context can also help us to better anticipate the flow of the conversation, understand the emotions conveyed and contribute more effectively to the discussion. Without this information, we feel left out or confused, which eventually will lead to frustration and miscommunication.

While guiding a blind person like me, let us hold onto your arm and follow you. If there is a narrow space, move your arm behind your back for us to walk behind you in a straight line. If you come across an obstacle or stairs, stop for a moment to let us know. **Tell us whether the steps go up or downand let us find the handrail and position the edge of the first step before proceeding. DON'T take hold of us by our hand, arm, or shoulder and try to maneuver us.**

While we may require assistance in certain situations, one may not always assume that we are incapable because we cannot see. As visually impaired and blind community, we learn to do some astonishing things without our sight and we are often more independent than one may believe. We often don't need help with basic tasks that usually one would rely on their sight to perform.

Therefore, I perceive visual impairment as a mere physical challenge. By no means do I see it as a weakness or the end of my glory. And I don't believe that being blind is anyone's identity. I am as powerful, unbeatable and capable as anybody else.

When you come across someone like me, instead of feeling sorry, I encourage you to reflect on your assumptions towards individuals with different abilities. This can help to identify and challenge standards of society that may contribute to negative interactions with us.

We are open to curious questioning about our situation. You may generally not know how to be with people like us, or might want to understand us better. Thus, it is totally fine for you to ask us about our lives and how our experiences are. We can share valuable ideas if you ask us. Just be friendly, include us in social activities and talk to us.

Unfortunately, even the most outgoing and friendly blind people

like me, cannot always make the first move. That's why,when you want to communicate with us, speak to us! Not the person we are with. There is nothing that irritates us more than people assuming we are incapable of having a conversation. We don't enjoy being treated as if we are incompetent also. So speak directly to us, rather than our attendant.

DO introduce yourself, especially when entering a room.

Don't say, "Do you know who I am?"

Don't shout at us while talking, we are not deaf. We can't see sure, but in reference with chapter 1, we do have fine hearing.

I like being Touched on my arm, or being called by my name, when someone is addressing me. This lets me know you are speaking to me, and not someone else in the room. Although like anyone else, even I do not like being touched excessively.

In hindsight, I may enjoy certain feelings, if not my full sight.

I am as fascinated with my environment as any other human. Yes! I like exploring new places, go to the movies or even the music concerts, try out new eating places and even indulge in adventure activities like trekking, jumping or diving etc.

This tendency mainly depends on the personality types of individuals. Some of us are reserved and think about our alone time more, while Others excitedly hunt for various experiences.

Moreover, blindness does not define our identity or limit our ability to lead fulfilling lives. Many blind individuals have successful careers, hobbies and relationships.

Just apply little sensitivity and open mindedness when

interacting with us, as you may well make our day. And you never know? You might just find yourself a new friend as well.

CHAPTER THREE

HOW THE BLIND READS

People often think of blindness as an all-or-nothing condition. They believe that we either have perfect sight or no sight at all. But that's not really true. There are many different levels of blindness. Some of us have trouble seeing clearly, while others have blind spots but can see other things well. Most of us who are visually impaired fall somewhere in between. Very few are completely blind.

Although the reality is that there are countless ways to be officially blind.

Visual impairment can come in many different forms. Some of us can read large print, while others can only see light and shadows, and some can't see anything at all. However, most of us can still see some things. Only a few of us have absolutely no sight. It's important to know that many people who are registered as blind can still see a little bit. But, unfortunately, not many people are aware of this.

Since I have low vision, or can be called visually impaired also, this is a different venture for me than it is for the average -vision individual.

I remember when I was sitting with a low-vision specialist right after being diagnosed with RP, he kept telling me that I must use the text-to-speech software on my computer. "But wouldn't Braille be better?" my father asked him. "he can hear me, so he can hear the computer, he explained to us. I argued that it wouldn't be easy for me, and I'd most likely end up missing words and get tired, but he still insisted that it was the best way to achieve literacy.

Fortunately, I followed his advise and learned "JAWS". With this software, students who are blind are able to access print material on a computer screen and it is for the school to purchase a screen reading software program. Screen reading software, like JAWS, reads the information on the computer screen. Students can use the word processing programs, calculators, internet and access other printed material without having to see the screen. Right now I'm about 70 to 80 percent up on my old reading speed, and I'm quite proud of myself.

What is RP?

Retinitis Pigmentosa is a genetic eye disorder that causes progressive degeneration of the cells in the retina. This can lead to symptoms such as night blindness, a decreased ability to see in dimly lit environments, and a loss of peripheral vision.

As the condition progresses, it can also affect central vision, making it difficult to see fine details and read small print.

That's me!

During my school days when RP(Retinitis Pigmentosa) started attacking my vision, there was quite a bit of pretending to read a book while staring into blurry and smudged ink! Nobody can possibly read with that low a vision, but I was so stuck with the conventional ways of reading that I couldn't detach myself only.

My point is that we people can be very rigid when it comes to substitute reading techniques.

It's important to recognize that we may have developed our own methods for accessing and interpreting information over time, which can become deep-rooted and familiar to us. These techniques may include reading through Braille, learning through audio books and accessing E-books through screen readers.

Over years, I have realized that it's best to use a combination of all.

E-books and audiobooks are two different formats for delivering written content to readers. The main difference between e-books and audiobooks is the way in which the content is consumed.

E-books are electronic versions of traditional books that can be read on devices such as e-readers, tablets, smartphones, or computers. They E-books are text-based and designed to be read through a screen reader, and we can even control the pace at which we read.

On the other hand, audiobooks are audio recordings of books that can be listened to on various devices, including smartphones, tablets, or dedicated audiobook players. Audiobooks are narrated by professional voice artists and can also include sound effects and music.

The choice between e-books and audiobooks depends on personal preferences and circumstances.

Not everyone can have financial access to expensive devices like computers and scanners, that's why majority have to rely on audio books as an alternative means to access printed material. It can help a learner access information with no trouble, but I want to inform you here, a blind person just listening to books on cassette or in song format on a music device is not enough to be called a literate.

It is important to understand that literacy is generally defined as the ability to read and write. Audio-based learning doesn't necessarily involve reading or typing on a computer, , so in that sense, it can be argued that it is not a form of literacy.

However, it is important to note that audio-based learning can still be a valuable form of education and can provide many benefits. For example, it can be a useful tool for language learning, as it allows learners to hear and practice proper pronunciation and accent. It can also be an alternate tool for individuals like me, who like reading while we are travelling.

With time, I have evolved to retain information through listening rather than reading. It's just a matter of practice, a lot of practice.

Using a screen reader requires us to learn many keyboard commands and shortcuts, as well as how to customize the settings to meet our specific needs. It's also important to have a good understanding of the accessibility features of different applications and websites, and how to work with them in combination with the screen reader.

Overall, while practice is certainly important in learning to use a screen reader, it's not the only factor. A combination of training, familiarity with the software and knowledge of accessibility features is necessary to become capable in using a screen reader.

Ultimately, while audio-based learning may not fit the strict definition of literacy, it is still a valuable form of education and can provide many benefits to us.

Some people may argue about the best way to teach blind students, but it's important to find the method that works best for each of us individually.

We often face a limited choice of "E-books". books are mostly available in audio tapes. Preparing eBooks is a difficult process which involves time and lot of effort. Although waiting times have decreased dramatically for E-books with the help of growing technology.

Some of us who read Braille have noticed that it's getting harder to find Braille books than before because most of us are using audio books instead. New technology is making it easier for us to read, but it also means that older ways of reading, like Braille, are not as popular anymore.

Therefore, each one of us, blind or low-vision, choose whichever reading technique fits our needs the best: visual, auditory, or Braille.

CHAPTER FOUR

OUR RACE AGAINST TIME

Our race against time is an expression that summarizes the challenges that we, as individuals face on day to day basis. It means that we have to work hard to get things done every day, like finishing tasks and achieving goals, while also dealing with problems caused by our disability. It can be difficult to balance everything, but we have to try our best to keep up with time.

At university, I found accessing books really difficult, as students usually have no time and therefore I didn't get much voluntary help or support in browsing through the library. one has to make all the required books available for himself in either e-text, audio or brail as the university doesn't care enough to work that much for 1% of people like us. .

It I had a print copy of the book with me, I found myself just at the beginning of the battle.

And because there were very few options of special places who would have catered to my requirements, I was left with doing it myself.

After spending many hours and money in first getting the book

Xeroxed and then scanning it with my own hands, is when I used to get ready for studying the same. By then my contemprories run far ahead of me and I used to suffer with no fault of my own. Only if I had it already available in e-text, I wouldn't have felt that emotional pain during my education. Although, doing it ourselves is absolutely not what I'm trying to market, as this involves a lot of money and only a very few blind students can practically afford to take up this challenge. Lack of a strong family support is also responsible in many cases of disappointment.

Another challenge is taking down class notes during the professor's lectures. Few of the same gadgets that students use to listen to recorded texts such as CD players, MP3 players, tape recorders, iPhones and iPads can also be used to record a lesson for studying, notetaking purposes and for writing assignments. But before recording classroom lessons or instructions, we also have to get permission from the university because some colleges have strict rules against it.

As blind students, we have to face many different challenges when it comes to accessing higher education. Despite the government's initiatives to provide equal opportunities to all students, we often experience a lack of support and equal place in colleges.

One of our biggest challenge is the lack of access to materials in accessible formats. Many reference materials, online resources and even textbooks are not available in formats that can be accessed by blind students. This means that we often have to rely on our classmates or teachers to read out material to us, which is not always possible.

Many colleges don't have enough people who know how to help us. They also don't have necessary gadgets that can help us learn, like computers with a text to speech program which reads out loud. Because of this, it's hard for us to take part in class and we struggle with assignments and tests. After all, not every blind student can afford a computer and that's why financial barrier has become another big challenge in accessing higher education. The cost of tuition fees, accommodation, textbooks, and other materials can be a significant burden for blind students and their families, particularly for those from low-income households. Many of us face lack of information on the application process, scholarships, and other resources that can help us access higher education. This can be particularly challenging for blind students who also are the first in their families to attend college, as they may not have access to the same level of support and guidance as other students.

Discrimination is another battle that awaits us. This can take many forms, including racial, gender, or socioeconomic biases, and can additionally make it difficult for some of us to receive the support we need to succeed once we are enrolled. Mistreatment based on our disability is unacceptable and can have a significant impact on our well-being and self-esteem. Although, I personally give biased people a benefit of doubt, because their behavior towards us can be shaped due to their own beliefs, experiences and preferences, which can lead to their mistreatment and misunderstandings in our direction.

Besides all this, people around us like classmates and teachers don't always know about our difficulties and may not be able to help us. This can make us feel left out at times.

As a result, it's like we're not starting from the same point as everyone else in the race.

Special institutes are not rewarding enough due to lack of competence in peers. And regular institutes never place us right with peers.

Therefore, only the tough ones survive, and the rest fall apart.

It is important to know that disability is not our defining characteristic. It simply refers to an impairment that may affect our daily life in various ways, but it does not diminish our worth or value as a human being.

Many public fascilities like transportation systems aren't set up for our needs. This means it takes longer for us to do things. Sometimes, we can't even use these places at all because they don't have things like signs we can touch or announcements we can hear. This makes it hard for us to be a part of society like everyone else.

We also have to deal with a lot of emotional issues because of how people treat us when we're blind. They may think we can't do things or are not important, hence it becomes difficult to feel good about ourselves.

Regardless of these challenges, I'm glad that many of us have shown notable resilience and creativity in overcoming these obstacles. Training and education programs have enabled us to acquire skills that allow us to lead independent and productive lives.

We have also found backing in support groups and organizations who voice our rights and promote awareness about the challenges we face.

However, it is important for all educational institutions to bring their attention to providing equal opportunities and accessibility support for students with disabilities. This includes physical accessibility, such as wheelchair ramps and accessible restrooms, as well as academic accommodations, such as assistive technology and note-taking support.

Governments, organizations, and businesses just need to make sure that buildings, transportation, and public places can be used by everyone, including people with disabilities.

CHAPTER FIVE

THE MENTAL AND EMOTIONAL CONFLICTS

The Emotional Side of Losing One's Vision is a different experience for different individuals and their families. it's the change that's the hard part, not the vision loss itself.

People born blind don't have to struggle with this particular phase. Others like me who lose their sight later in life do.

When I lost my ability to see, I was very scared of loosing my identity as well. I was dependent on seeing things to understand and losing that made me feel completely detached. I was struggling to adjust to my new normal. Every day was a challenge as I tried to navigate the world with my new found reality.

My parent's suffering was no less, it certainly was a hard time for me and my family.

I still remember how hesitant they were of how to tell family members and friends about my visual impairment. They never put it on display, but I'm sure they were wondering how my condition is going to affect my future. I learned it in the beginning only that not everyone is going to respond sensitively. Each person who learned about my condition reacted differently. Some people said just what we wanted to hear in the moment, but others missed the mark and said many disturbing things.

Whether we were talking with friends, family or complete strangers, there were times when we were really uncomfortable, puzzled and sometimes even angry at people's reactions.

Despite all this, we also assumed that most people have very little or no experience with vision loss, and so, they are unsure how to react to us.

Nobody is a mind reader after all, and together as a family, we understood.

Being a teenager, I was always scared that I would cause problems for my family and friends because of my disability. I was worried that I wouldn't be able to do normal things and that people might treat me unfairly. I was also disturbed about loosing sight of my dreams and other financial troubles my disability might cause.

This created a sense of loneliness within me, which was very difficult to deal with. After all, vision is the most important of the senses and is necessary for day-to-day functioning.

The thought of living in a world without the capability to see can be devastating, and this fear can create a sense of uncertainty and anxiety.

Pretty awful, uh?

Honestly, It's not that awful. It's life and we learn how to deal with it. We actually don't lose as much independence as one

might think.

The good news is that there are many ways to overcome these fears and insecurities. Learning survival strategies, such as relaxation techniques and meditation can also be useful in reducing stress and anxiety.

I can speak with some authority on this matter since I have retinitis pigmentosa(RP) for many years. Coping up with the same has become a routine now. I should have rather started off with acceptance. Accepting my blindness could have been the most important first step. This I regret till date as it accounts to many years of going through the discomfort of pretending.

Acceptance doesn't mean we have to like it, but acknowledging it can help us move forward and focus on what we can truly control.

Slowly, I began to see things differently. I learned to use my other senses to explore my surroundings, and I discovered that I could still live a full and happy life. With time, my fear turned into acceptance, and I realized that blindness was just a part of who I was, not a limitation.

I truly started off by practicing self-care, making time for activities that brought me joy and helped me relax, such as staying active, meditating and spending time in nature. Taking care of myself by getting enough sleep, eating a healthy diet, and working out regularly has always helped me feel better mentally and emotionally.

So, how we feel and believe about ourselves is influenced by how we behave towards ourselves.

But it is important to recognize that our behavior is not always conscious, and we may not be aware of how it is impacting our self-perception.

That's why, I always stay positive. Focusing on the things I can do, rather than the things I can't. This also includes Setting goals, both short term and long term, and celebrating my own achievements.

Another negative part of losing one's sight is the feeling of incompetence. As someone who's naturally not organized, the new way of interacting with the world can get tricky. I've cracked or broken more than half of my set of drinking glasses by dropping or knocking them over. I've walked into people by mistake. I've stepped on my pet dog too many times to mention. The street dogs have been accidentally treated by me as footballs and I'm scared that one of them holds back a grudge.

As I tried to rectify each mistake, I only seem to make things worse, leading to a series of humorous and embarrassing situations.

But, constantly challenging negative thoughts have been my greatest weapon against them. Negative thoughts are normal, but they can be destructive if they become inescapable. I have learn to challenge negative thoughts by asking myself if they are even genuine.

Considering alternative ways to look at the same situation over and over gave me a sense of Having something to work towards, which helped me in staying motivated and focused.

My achievements in life, education, jobs or my entrepreneurial journey were directly proportional to the expectations that people around had of me. The more talented and capable my parents believed I was , the more I made attempts to excel.

I'm the kind of person who hates lacking ability. I like doing things well to a certain degree, I've done many things well. At

times, I feel like a failure at adjusting. When I lose something for a countless number of times, I find criticizing myself for not being better at being blind. Despite my best efforts, I often used to find myself constantly making mistakes and facing unexpected challenges, leading to a series of humorous misunderstandings and misadventures.

I'm getting better, though. I haven't broken or even cracked a glass in months. The dogs now know to avoid me when I'm moving swiftly. Adjusting or rather Adapting is a much slower process than I ever expected, but it's moving in the right direction.

I have finally understood the importance of coming out of the closet and sharing. Hiding from the world is the worst form of recovery and that's why it's important to share.

Overall, coming out to others is a personal decision that can have a positive impact on one's life. It takes courage and strength to be true to our self but eventually, it leads to a sense of choice and liberty.

Just remember, everyone's journey is different and there is no "right" way to do it.

The path to acceptance is a slow one, full of broken glasses and annoyed dogs, but I'm getting there.

CHAPTER SIX

CONTROVERSIALLY NAVIGATING THE WORLD

Legal blindness qualifies one for certain services from the government, including the right to use a white cane or a service animal. Moreover, legality applies to people who are blind or have low vision.

There are three main navigation techniques that blind and low-vision folks use: a white cane, guide dogs or nothing. There are some political and personal preferences involved in one's choice depending on which part of the world's blind population we're a part of.

Navigating the world as a blind person can be a scary task. Every day, we are faced with the challenge of finding our way around in a sighted world. Amid all this chaos, one of the most valuable tools for us is, the white cane. It's a simple yet powerful tool that allows blind people like me to navigate our surroundings with confidence and independence. It is a long, thin stick with a rounded tip that can detect obstacles and changes in landscapes. Like any other utility tool, even The white cane has come a long way since its introduction. With advancements in technology and design, it is becoming more multipurpose and effective than ever. There are now electronic white canes that use sensors to detect obstacles and provide audio feedback, and there are other designs with built-in GPS and other navigation tools.

For me, the white cane is a lifeline. It allows me to travel safely and independently and explore even unfamiliar places.

It also serves as a symbol of the blind community and is an accepted symbol of disability.

The white cane has had a deep impact on the lives of visually impaired individuals around the world. It has provided us with a sense of independence and freedom that was once unattainable, enabling us to live a more fulfilling and meaningful life.

However, the journey to becoming expert in using a white cane can be a difficult and frustrating task.

It's a process that takes time and practice. At first, the cane can feel uncomfortable and unmanageable because of the unique sensations it provides. We often go through a period of adjustment when we first start using a cane, as we learn to interpret the information that it provides and to make decisions based on that information.

Another challenge is dealing with unexpected obstacles and changes in terrain. We often encounter obstacles such as stairs, edges and uneven surfaces, which can be difficult to detect. Navigating these hurdles requires a combination of skill, self-confidence and awareness, as well as a willingness to ask for help when required.

We also face a number of practical concerns. For example, the cane can be difficult to use in crowded or busy situations, where it may be knocked out of our hand or bounce into other people. It can also be difficult to use the cane in extreme weather, such as rain or snow, when the ground may be slippery.

On top of this, dealing with the perceptions and attitudes of others is a constant and exhausting job for us. Many people are unaware of how to interact with someone like me, who is using a cane, and may treat us with pity. While others may simply not know how to behave around us, and may unintentionally make things more difficult.

Being a visually impaired individual who relies on a white cane, it is crucial for us to exercise patience towards others and to educate them. This can be inspiring, and is an important step in encouraging greater awareness and understanding of blindness.

But learning to trust using a white cane is the mother of all challenges for us. We are reluctant to rely on the white cane, as we fear it will make us appear more disabled than we actually are. It takes time and training to build the confidence needed to use the white cane effectively.

Despite these encounters, the white cane remains an invaluable tool for blind people, enabling us to live more independently and to participate fully in our communities. With practice and determination, we can learn to use the cane with confidence and skill, and to navigate the world with comfort and independence.

I have eventually learned to adapt with the white cane by developing techniques and strategies to navigate challenging environments. Like, appointing the cane more frequently and using my other senses to supplement the use of my cane. I have Practiced using my white cane in different environments to improve my skills. Starting off with familiar routes and gradually increasing the difficulty level.

I Just worked upon the belief in myself along with my ability to navigate with the white cane and approached each challenge with the determination to succeed.

At the end of the day, the white cane is more than just a tool. It is a symbol of our strength, resilience and willpower. It represents our ability to overcome challenges and to live our lives on our own terms, with dignity and pride. Whether we are walking down the street or exploring a new place, the white cane is a constant companion, helping us to navigate the world with grace and confidence.

Another way of navigating is through service animals. Many overseas friends and family who watched that particular programmed on the Discovery Channel about The Guide Dogs, pushed me to get a dog. Living in their own zones, they seem to feel more comfortable with the idea of a seeing-eye dog for me.

I have always courteously declined my relative's involvement and have tried to seek advice from someone else who may have a better understanding of my needs. I believe that only I have the right to make decisions that are in my best interest, and that includes looking for advice from those who understand and respect my visual impairment.

In my defence to my overseas family and friends, laws and regulations regarding service animals vary worldwide.

Some of them think that it's a cool way to get a very well-trained pet. But it is not that simple in India, keeping in mind the conditions of roads, pedestrian paths and more over, the traffic sense in the common man.

But there is no denying that Companionship offered by a pet helps reduce anxiety, depression, and loneliness. The animals

may also lead to increased interaction with other people as they are seen as "ice breakers" to a conversation with something to talk about. Therefore, Meeting people and socializing is easier, and people are more likely to be watchful around us when there is a service animal present.

In many cases, service animals offer a life changing experience. They are better than long canes when one is in an new place. The animal directs the right path, instead of nudging around. Over all, service animals make the experience of the unknown more comforting.

With a cane, dark glasses or a seeing-eye animal, people notice us because we are different. But, A white cane can be put away at any time. It doesn't poop, shed or require vet visits. Nobody wants to pet a cane either. Guide dogs are wonderful but have a lot of risk involved.

In the end, it's a personal choice dependent on one's lifestyle and needs.

For me, it's a symbol of pride and a statement of my determination to overcome challenges and live life to the fullest.

CHAPTER SEVEN

THE WHITE CANE

As simple as the white cane may be, it still requires training. There are different grips, arcs and contacts. We hold and move it in different ways, depending on how many people are around us, and our familiarity of the area, among other factors. The white cane gives us a lot of information, but there are a few things that surprise us like chairs and tables.

It's true that using a white cane can make people notice that we have trouble seeing. This can make us feel like other people are paying more attention to us, which can make us feel uncomfortable or embarrassed when we're out in public.

Some of us feel ashamed only because many have wrong ideas about not being able to see well. But we need to talk about these ideas and explain that it's not anyone's fault if one can't see well. It's not something to be embarrassed about.

I believe that using a white cane can also be empowering, as it allows me to navigate my environment more safely and confidently. It may also serve as a signal to others that I may need assistance or accommodation, which can lead to greater accessibility and inclusivity in public spaces.

This is good and bad.

I usually get excellent customer service at restaurants, stores, and offices with employees going out of their way to make sure my needs are met. I'm very grateful for these employees. Most people are willing to give me directions. I get on first on flights and sometimes get placed in the first row and at times, I'm even lucky enough to get promoted to the Business Class. Kindness has been the general rule but, As with any rule, there are exceptions. Some people stare or back away from me as if I'm infectious. They probably think I don't see them, but I do.

If we are using a white cane, it is generally a visible indication that we have a visual impairment. It is important to understand that a white cane is not just a tool for navigating the physical environment, but it is also a symbol that represents our identity and communicates to others that we have a disability.

While it is true that some of us may try to conceal our disability, using a white cane would make that difficult. However, it is important to respect the decision on how we choose to disclose our disability or not. Everyone has the right to choose how and when they share information about themselves.

The focus should be on welcoming everyone, regardless of the ability status or whether or not our disability is visible.

But my cane is more than just a tool for navigation. it is also an extension of my personality. I use my white cane as a fashion accessory, customizing it to match my outfits and personal style.

I would often wrap my cane with brightly colored ribbons, or add hangings and charms and even paint it with sophisticated patterns. Friends and family often compliment me on my unique style and creativity.

This gives me a sense of pride in my ability to turn something functional into something fashionable.

If we have a constructive self-image and feel confident in ourselves, we may display a certain level of positivity that can be attractive to others.

I also find learning every detail about my home environment very interesting. I prefer placing Large obstacles such as tables and chairs in one location to prevent injury. I also ensure that each member of my household is carefully keeping walkways clear and all items in chosen locations, and providing me with evenly distributed lighting in all areas of the house.

My family ensures a safe and supportive environment for me by making such lifestyle changes.

But when I'm outdoors, people watch me. Since I'm no longer unidentified, I feel constant pressure not to stumble or fall, which is tough. It's a disappointing feeling sometimes. the sense that I can't make a mistake, that I can't trip.

I often find myself missing my secrecy the most. But it is also nice to get in front of the queues.

Sometimes we get to avail reduced entry fees as some public places offer reduced or free admission for us. Other times we enjoy priority seating which may be located closer to the entrance, or have extra space to accommodate our white canes.

But, we often have to give up our privacy while receiving help and support from others. It can have negative consequences, such as the loss of personal information and the potential for exploitation. Although, volunteers are typically expected to act with honesty, kindness, and respect towards the individuals they are serving, yet there are incidences where blind people have been victims of a crime.

Yes! We can be victims of crime just like any other person. In fact, we're particularly more exposed to certain types of crimes because we cannot see our surroundings or potential threats as easily.

That's why it becomes even more important for us to be aware of our surroundings and to take precautions when out in public. This can include traveling in well-lit areas, avoiding isolated places, and being conscious of people around us. Total awareness and keeping all our senses at full alert can teach us how to use our cane effectively, how to identify potential hazards, and how to stay safe in different situations.

We can also use a specialized cane and other assistive devices that can help increase our safety and privacy. For example, some canes are designed to collapse or fold up, making them less noticeable when not in use. Additionally, there are devices that get attached to a cane or clothing and can be triggered to produce a loud alarm if we encounter a threat.

Still, it is important to remember that being blind does not make us less deserving of protection from harm. We face a unique set of challenges and difficulties in our daily lives, and it is important to recognize and address these challenges in order to create a safe society. By providing accessible information, creating inclusive environments, and promoting awareness and understanding of our needs, can ensure that we have equal opportunities to participate fully in society. It is important that we work together to create a world that is accessible and harmless for everyone, regardless of ability or disability.

Moreover, there are ways to balance privacy and social connection, such as selectively sharing personal information with trusted individuals only.

At the end of the day, I refuse to be defined by my disability and instead believe in embracing it as a part of who I am.

OUR CHALLENGES

Blindness also causes significant social challenges, usually in relation to the activities in which we cannot participate. All too frequently, blindness affects our ability to perform many job duties, which severely limits our employment opportunities. This not only affects our finances, but also our self-esteem. Blindness may also cause difficulties with participating in activities outside of a workplace, such as sports and practical studies. Many of these social challenges also limit our ability to meet new people, and this only adds to low self-esteem.

However, it's important to note that every person's experiences are exclusive, and some blind individuals like me, can have strong social networks and feel confident in our social interactions.

While mentoring my blind students, I try to address the issue of low self-esteem.

Helping them Explore opportunities for socialization and connection within the blind community has generated many positive results and success stories.

Yet, self-esteem can be influenced by many factors beyond social interaction also. Overall, it will be wrong to say that conditions of anxiety or depression come in a package deal with vision loss and can be ignored.

But there may be differences still in confidence levels, between people who were born blind and those who became blind later in life.

Though, it's not necessarily helpful to generalize about the confidence levels of blind individuals based on this because individual experiences can vary significantly.

Other factors such as personality, support networks, life experiences, and mental health can all play a role in shaping up confidence levels.

Still we all go through many unique experiences, no matter which side of the hedge we fall. If one is born blind, it does not feel like anything. We do not see black. We see nothing. To us it is completely normal, as we do not know any other way of life. It is like asking what it feels like to be white, black, or any other race. It just is who we are.

People describing things to us in terms of color gives us an idea, but it is still based on our thoughts and not what color really it is. For example, we know a banana is yellow. So when you say there goes a yellow car, we think banana.

But if one goes blind as an adult, like I did, it is very weird in the beginning. I do see black and understand colours, yet I know I am missing things.

How our dreams look like is another unique experience.

Yes, blind people do see dreams. However, the content of our dreams may differ from that of sighted people.

Dreams of people who were born blind may involve other sensory experiences such as touch, smell, and sound.

Late blind's dreams may still include visual imagery, as their brain has already formed visual memories.

It is important to note that not all blind people experience dreams in the same way, just like how not all sighted individuals have the same dream experiences.

I used to be a sighted individual in my dreams initially. But, over time, I started to dream as I was blind. This is because my brain started accepting the blindness and it was my reality. Given enough time, it becomes normal, and we stop thinking about it.

Although, The script of dreams can also be influenced by our past experiences and memories, as well as our current thoughts and emotions.

I remember reading this somewhere that, dreams are a creation of the brain's activity during the REM (rapid eye movement) phase of sleep, and this is not dependent on visual input.

However, there are things I miss while I'm awake, like looking at my family.

I remember watching their faces about 20 years back. Their same image flash in my head today when I hear their voice. They try to describe the changes to me, and it helps because I do have a previous reference point.

Yes, We learn to perceive people's appearance and map out the world differently. For example, instead of reading the street signs, I count the number of intersections now. I have stopped using the red lights to know when to cross the road, but look or

listen for the traffic flow. Many of us also try to use GPS systems, but since it's usually inaccurate in India, I don't use GPS for walking. Sensory landmarks such as a distinctive smell, familiar noises around or bumps in roads orient me to the world around me therefore, Memory becomes crucial.

Sometimes I use a human guide. I hate to do this, not just because it limits my independence, but because most people are terrible at it. They'll grab me and proceed to drag making me stumble and disoriented. They'll forget to stop before a step, so I tend to trip. Even with instruction, guiding someone else is a sensitive exercise that not a lot of people have a talent for. Try and let us lead the way as often as possible, correcting only if our safety is in danger. This will give us confidence and the ability to travel without an aide.

We may rely on sighted folks for a few things, but there is no evidence to suggest that people with sight are inherently smarter than us. Intellect is a complex characteristic that cannot be concentrated to a single factor.

However, it is true that blind people often develop exceptional skills in areas such as memory and auditory processing. Due to our finely tuned dependence on these abilities, we compensate for our lack of sight.

It is a result of the brain's ability to reorganize and adapt to new sensory inputs.

For example, blind people have been shown to have better spatial memory and navigation skills than sighted individuals because we rely on other senses such as hearing and touch to navigate our environment. Our heavy reliance on sound to understand our surroundings makes us ahead of the curve.

However, it is important to note that these skills are not universal among all blind individuals, and that some sighted individuals may also possess exceptional skills in these areas.

All in all, intelligence is a multilayered trait, and cannot be reduced to a simple comparison between sighted and blind individuals.

CHAPTER NINE

WHY DO WE HIDE

Honesty from the get-go is what I support.

But I've been a hypocrite myself, because for years, I've lied.

Not directly, but in front of my family, others and all of the rest. Little white lies And, when you put them together, don't look so little anymore. The lies have been crucial, I've told myself, in order to protect a secret. A big, absurd secret I've been keeping about myself since before it became obvious.

I'm blind.

I know, it sounds shocking. There's no way a person could be blind without other people noticing. But contrary to popular belief, blindness isn't always a black and white kind of thing. Right now, I'm legally blind, creeping a little closer to flat-out-blind every day. I don't wear sunglasses and I don't have a service dog, though my vision has deteriorated to the point where a mobility cane is very helpful.

Of course, the cane would be a pretty noticeable clue as to my secret so I've managed without it. Until I couldn't do without it.

So sure, I see the world the way you would if you were looking through peepholes covered in white cream.

It's super inconvenient.

But what's even more inconvenient than our blindness is trying to hide it.

Over the years, as I've lost more and more vision, it's taken more and more time and energy to hide this fact, and as I have grown from being a student to a Business man and then a part time teacher for the blind individuals, time and energy is exactly what I don't have.

I can very well compare my situation with any given human being with this condition because In the beginning, our vision loss isn't a lie, just a personal detail we like to keep close to us like any other of our dark secrets.

I was particularly fearful about people finding it because then I'd be pitied or bombarded with sympathy talks, or defined by my fore coming tragedy.

Since my disease progressed slowly, my vision was unaffected for a very long time. But, as time passed and my little blind spots grew, the fact of my vision loss became more noticeable.

None of us actively choose to keep our blindness secret. we just don't tell the truth about it, and the lie grows all on its own.

I had a vision where I was able to recognize, but I found it difficult to pretend that I could see beyond my actual abilities.

This sentiment could apply to a variety of situations. For example, you may have a dream or goal that you want to pursue, but you may struggle with admitting to yourselves or others that you don't have all the skills or knowledge necessary to achieve it.

In such a case, I advocate accepting the truth of the limitations. Acceptance is always difficult, but it can also be an important step towards growth and progress.

Alternatively, this statement could also relate to physical or sensory limitations, like in my case. Admitting to myself and others that I cannot see correctly was challenging.

By acknowledging my limitations and being honest about what I could, and couldn't do, I definitely would have moved forward with greater clarity and self-awareness.

Overall, this statement suggests that it can be easier to accept the truth of a situation than to try and pretend that it is something else, even if that truth is difficult to face.

It is important to note that our individual experiences with low vision are different. There may be reasons unknown as to why some of us may choose to keep our condition a secret.

For me, it was people's Perception of my condition as my weakness or incapacity. This was like labelling me much below my self worth.

As a result, I had my days of embarrassment while hiding my condition in college as I had experienced negative reactions from my school mates in the past. I was worried that even they would judge me or think less of me if I revealed my condition.

But the cause of these hiding tendencies have their roots around the time when I was diagnosed with RP. During the first few years, I struggled to come to terms with my diagnosis, and was not ready to admit it. I felt that keeping my condition a secret will allow me to maintain a sense of normalcy or avoid confronting the reality of my situation.

Yes, accepting my vision loss was a difficult process, but it was the best decision towards living a fulfilling life. Hiding or pretending was exhausting, both physically and emotionally. My acceptance allowed me to explore new ways of doing things and find solutions to the challenges I used to face. However, It's important to remember that acceptance doesn't mean giving up on our goals and dreams. With determination and will power, we can continue to pursue our passions and live a full and rewarding life. My success today is the result of a combination of factors, including perseverance, adaptability and even luck. While willpower helped me in overcoming obstacles, it was important to also have the willingness to learn and adapt as circumstances changed. Additionally, social support, mentorship, access to resources and opportunities also played a critical role in shaping my destiny.

Therefore, blindness does not control one's ability to achieve wealth or success.

But, my physical appearance and how I look at myself has been a annoying problem till a very long time.

Today, a surprising side-effect of my vision loss is the readjustment of my perception of my appearance.

If one can't see himself clearly in the mirror ... what happens?

I'm an ordinary person in the sense that I had hints of insecurities about my body. I'd look in the mirror and see things that I disliked. I attached a fair part of my self-confidence to what I saw in the mirror and got satisfied.

After a period of deep insecurity about my physical appearance, I began a new relationship with my own body. Unable to see myself all that well, I've begun to focus more on how I feel. Do I feel strong? smart? Ugly? Pretty? These things are all internal.

Now that I gym and swim regularly, wear trendy clothes, I feel far prettier and more at home in my own body than I ever did before. I'm discovering that I quite like the body I live in.

I don't think about the imperfections because I can't see them. Ironically, seeing my body only in a blurry and distorted form has made me appreciate it more. Funny how the world works for us.

Being blind does not limit our potential for achieving our dreams. With dedication, honesty and a positive attitude, anyone, regardless of their physical disabilities, can achieve their dreams.

Blind people like me often face additional challenges, but it does not mean that we cannot achieve our goals.

It is easy to become discouraged when faced with challenges, but I refuse to give up. I have understood during the course of my struggles that success requires perseverance and resilience. I never let my disabilities define me. Instead, I focus on my strengths and work tirelessly every day to achieve my goals.

Every morning is a new opportunity to start fresh, to forget the hurt from the previous day, and to move forward. It is very critical to understand that setbacks are a part of life.

Ultimately, success is not determined by one's circumstances, but by their willingness to work hard.

CHAPTER TEN

ME, MYSELF AND MOSTLY OTHERS

So, what *I* see is unique to me and my condition. No other blind person will see as I do.

My condition causes night blindness, gradual central vision loss, and in its advanced stages retinal issues. Even though it's a progressive condition, it progresses differently for everyone. My lower and upper fields of vision have been gone since mid teens. I have blind spots in the sides of my vision, but I can detect light and movement in my far peripheries. The funny thing is that I don't actually see the blind spots, my brain has reconfigured my visual perception to skip over them. So my brain is constantly tricking me.

Hence my claim, that no other blind person will see as I do

Each person's experience of blindness is unique and cannot be replicated by anyone else. This claim highlights the fact that blindness is not a standardized condition and that people who are blind may have different observations, experiences and coping strategies.

Blindness can result from a variety of causes like, disease, injury, genetics or aging. It can also vary in severity and nature. Some of us who are blind may have left over vision or may experience visual hallucinations, while others may rely on alternative senses such as touch, hearing, or smell to navigate the world around.

Therefore, it's possible that no two blind individuals will experience the world in the exact same way, as each of our opinions are influenced by our unique set of experiences, circumstances and personality.

I remember when I was just 16 years old, my RP began affecting the central part of my eyes, which is a somewhat unusual development that early. It affects color judgment and visual sharpness. As of right now, my eyes have vision left which is uncorrectable by glasses.

Everything seems out of focus. If a person is standing more than 2 feet away from me, his or her face is as blurry as in a smudged painting. Typically, I identify a familiar person by his profile and the way he talks. I can't recognize faces with much precision up close and I can't even see fine detail like small scars and roughness. So people all look like they have amazing skin. Bright light makes my vision worse. It seems like a thin white film is covering everything, making light-colored things almost glow. Often, harsh direct light will create shadows that confuse me, since the world becomes too visually complicated. Certain shadows might look like steps of a staircase since my distance awareness is basically zero.

The situation is similar for dim places. Everything goes gray or black if it's quite dark. I can't see depth or shadows in the night. It's just one big wall of black, dotted by streetlights.

However, I see quite well under the perfect conditions like, evenly distributed light of medium intensity with simple and high-contrast items plus relatively stationary people and things.

But, life rarely provides perfect conditions. I still feel traumatized remembering my ordeal at school and how it was far far away from being perfect.

My life after vision loss started off dealing with mistreatment I had to face from fellow students.

They would intentionally move chairs in my way, push me, misguide me to the wrong facilities and make fun of me. Sometimes, they would hit me as I was defenseless, just to have a laugh, spill cold water on me in winters or lock me up in restricted areas.

I was an easy target because for them, I was just a boy with week vision, like any other boy would have week muscles, or be loosely built, or have a short height.

Teachers and parents didn't understand different varieties of blindness due to lack of awareness back in late 90's, and therefore, I had no support.

After repeated complaints and no change in the bullying behavior, I felt discouraged and helpless. It did have a very deep impact on my mental health and the struggle only amplified.

I accepted every day bulleying as a routine of my life which stopped only on the weekends, or school holidays.

It is important for schools and communities to take steps to prevent and address bullying of all kinds, including bullying of visually impaired individuals like me.

Such harassment should never be accepted, and

Schools must work to educate students about all forms of disabilities and also the importance of treating others with empathy and respect. It is very critical for teachers and parents to be watchful for signs of bullying. This may include talking to the children involved, contacting parents or involving school authorities as needed.

They can establish clear policies and procedures for addressing bullying and consequences for those who engage in such behavior.

Channelizing rage in the right direction helped me from a very young age. Learning the skill to steer my anger in a healthy and productive way assisted me throughout my life. It helped me to express my emotions in a constructive way, manage stress and spreading awareness along with generating an atmosphere of positivity and inclusiveness all around.

Remember, it is natural to feel angry at times, but it is important to learn healthy ways of expressing and managing this emotion. With practice and persistence, all of us can learn to channelize our anger in a positive and productive way.

I've personally never let the words or actions of others bring me down.

It's also important to prioritize self-care and focus on building own sense of self-worth and self-esteem. One must not forget that we are valuable and deserving of respect.

At the end of the day, it is up to all of us to create safe and inclusive societies where all individuals, including visually impaired children, can prosper and feel supported.

Blind students should keep in mind that bullying is never okay, and there are resources available to help us address the situation and protect self now.

Over time, I've been able to forgive my bullies and let go of grudges

I have had towards them. Holding onto grudges could have been damaging to my mental health and general well-being. It takes a lot of strength and maturity to be able to forgive those who have wronged us, and it's important to remember that forgiveness is not about excusing their behavior or forgetting what happened, but rather about freeing ourselves from negative emotions and moving forward with our lives.

It's also worth noting that sometimes people act out of ignorance or lack of understanding, and it's not always a reflection of who they are as a person. Our visual impairment is a part of who we are, but it doesn't define us. By choosing to let go of any resentment we may have held towards our bullies, we are taking control of our own narrative and not allowing their actions to dictate our life.

I've had and will always Keep up my positive attitude and focus on being the best version of myself that I can be!

CHAPTER ELEVEN

MAKING CHOICES

My early diagnosis at age sixteen was equal parts a blessing and curse. Many people with RP aren't diagnosed until their early adulthood.

Knowing my vision would eventually finish into darkness, helped me make certain life decisions, mostly for the positive.

I'll let you into a little secret. Having your choices narrowed down to a few makes it easier to make a choice and be happy with the choice. If you have a surplus of choices, you're far more likely to get hung up on the superficial differences. Whereas, If you only have two, the differences are clearer and regret is minimized.

As a teenager, I faced the challenge of learning how to drive with great confusion and anxiety. I lived in an era where a car was a necessity. All of my friends were getting their licenses and I was just boiling in frustration. My father refused to let me drive, but through pure teenage stubbornness, I started lessons. I reasoned that my sight was still quite good, so it was all right.

When I began lessons, I began to consider the realities of my future for the first time. Behind the wheel of a sedan, I wondered if I would be self-aware enough to stop driving when I loose more and more vision, or before I hurt anyone.

The truth was no. I was too determined and willful to stop before the bitter end. I had to pay a high price before I could accept the reality.

So, my father had to give away his car for repair and I had to hand in my self-obtained driver's license for life.

It was difficult for me to come to terms with the impact of my declining vision on my ability to drive safely. It was important for me to recognize back then, that driving is a privilege and responsibility that requires a certain level of visual and cognitive ability to ensure the safety of myself and others on the road.

Although it was the most heart breaking decision to make, ultimately choosing to stop driving when my vision began to decline was a responsible choice.

It's never easy to give up something that we enjoy or rely on, but in this case, it was necessary for my safety and that of others.

Since then, I've used public transportation and took rides from friends and family. It's not a bad way to live. At least I don't have to think about auto insurance or car maintenance now.

Public transportation, cab sharing services and mobility training programs are a few resources and services available for blind individuals like us. Additionally, there are many assistive technologies available that can help make everyday tasks, including transportation, easier and more accessible.

Our safety, and the safety of those around us, is the most important consideration when it comes to driving. It takes maturity and responsibility to make difficult decisions like this, and today I'm proud of myself for recognizing the risks and taking steps to minimize them.

My forthcoming vision loss made my moral compass clear for me- Learn to be independent in a way that doesn't unnecessarily endanger others.

My vision loss also narrowed my career options, but eventually led me down the right path.

My father being a government employee conveniently let me entertain the idea of becoming the same. But after thinking about it more, I realized that it wasn't the most useful route, and would result in me doing something I didn't want to do.

So, I reassessed my talents, as insufficient as they were, and decided on a more language-based career path. In the back of my mind, I considered words to be a permanent part of my life, no matter what my sight was like. Words are words, in braille or text. Words and language were the ultimate equalizers, since people would only judge me by my words throughout my life.

My mother wanted me to entre law, and even I had planned that I would have enough time before I lost my sight to make myself successful. But because of lack of awareness and wrong notions of life, my plan fell apart. I learned that thinking that one can plan life is extremely foolish and arrogant. Life has a tendency to disregard all attempts to control it.

Soon I realized that I was more in love with just the idea of the law than the practice itself. What I was truly passionate about was writing and reading. So, I studied literature instead.

The thing about being blind is that generally, nobody really expects much from you in terms of earning power or achievement. **But with me, it was always more about what I expected of myself. So, I did what I liked doing and life fell on the right track for me.**

We must not limit our expectations for our careers based on disability. But rather focus on our strengths, interests, and goals, and pursue opportunities that align with those factors.

With advances in technology and increasing awareness, we now have more opportunities than ever before to pursue our career goals.

It's important to note, that not all people who are visually impaired are identified as disabled, and there is a wide range of individual experiences and perspectives on this issue.

I see blindness as a neutral or sometimes even positive aspect of my identity, while others may still feel that it poses significant challenges and limitations.

Ultimately, the most important thing is to respect different personalities and evaluate us on the basis of our self-determination and will power.

There are many encouraging signs which show people's changing perceptions about blind people, and that blindness is increasingly being seen as just a difference rather than a disadvantage.

The entire blind community has worked to challenge the idea that people with visual impairment are naturally disadvantaged and in need of fixing.

Instead, the focus has shifted to creating a more comprehensive society that values diversity and recognizes the unique contributions that people with disabilities can make.

CHAPTER TWELVE

Relearning How to Live Life

I have always been a dreamer with a vision for my life that was bigger than myself and I was more than willing to work hard to make it a reality. However, there was one thing that threatened to derail my plans; my declining vision!

As a child, I had always been someone with a week sight, but my vision had worsened significantly over the years. By the time I reached my early twenties, I was nearly blind. Doctors had told me that my vision would only continue to decline, and that there was little they could do to stop it.

When my vision tipped from a nuisance into a disability, I no longer knew what to do. Getting around became a strange maze full of confusing images and new rules. People began to interact with me differently, always approaching me and even grabbing me in public. I had no idea how to react or manage these things because I was new at being blind, but people expected me to know what to do.

Having my vision gradually finish meant that I was always chasing a moving target. I first used to adapt to a certain level of vision, learned how to overcome my difficulties, then adjust to my lifestyle, and boom! The situation used to change again. My vision became weaker and weaker every year

It felt like a weird evolutionary adaption game that was specially designed for me.

When I accepted that I was going blind, many things in my life seem accelerated. I started to think about my life as divided between before and after.

At first, I was devastated. How could I possibly achieve my dreams if I couldn't see?

I remember having long conversations with myself analyzing possibilities until a point, when I thought to myself, what if I worked harder than ever before, so that I could achieve everything I wanted to see before my vision was gone completely?

And with this newfound determination, I threw myself into hard work.

I began making choices based on collecting the maximum experiences as early as possible

I never had the illusion that there would be a next time because I knew that there'd never be.

It was all about now. I was very impatient.

This impatience has led me to do some pretty stupid and smart things.

I was beginning to use a screen reading software, and I worked long hours every day. I learned to use the software that could help me finally read and complete my education. Gradually, I became an expert in using accessibility features to make my computer work for me.

As time went on, my vision continued to decline, but I refused to let it stop me. I worked even harder, driven by the knowledge that every day could be my last chance to see the world as I knew it. And slowly but surely, my hard work began to pay off.

My initiatives were better than ever before. I had started to get recognition in colleges, and my name was becoming known. I even started my own company, with a team of system analysts who worked alongside for becoming profitable.

But I never forgot why I was working so hard. I wanted to see it all - the world, my family and my dreams before complete darkness. And so, I continued to work tirelessly, until I had achieved everything I had ever wanted.

In the end, my vision did fail completely, but I didn't let it get in the way of my dreams. Instead, I learned to navigate the world with other senses, relying on my memory and my sixth sense to guide me.

I can look back at my life with a certain level of satisfaction. It has been a hell of a ride so far.

I've interacted with all sorts of people, Deaf, blind, immigrants, rich, poor, smart, and not-so-smart.

It amuses me when people assume that their lives are constant. I always knew mine wasn't, so I've taken risks accordingly. I, however, tried to be smart about risks. I never took risks that I thought would bring more long-term pain than momentary pleasure.

Of course, lowered risk aversion also leads to some stupidity as vision loss has a tendency of bringing out unwelcome changes in our personalities.

And I have no shame in admitting that I lost myself for a little while.

I considered college my last shot at pure carefreeness, so I partied my little heart out.

Most people would have described me as good-natured, quick to smile and laugh, and even a heartthrob. I was the one whom people spilled their guts to. Don't get me wrong. I was and am not a saint. I've been also known to hold grudges and say hurtful things once someone has crossed a certain line.

But when my vision suddenly tanked without warning, a lot of those things changed. I didn't smile as often. My temper shrank. I became a different person for a little while. A person even I didn't particularly liked.

I was used to success. I performed well academically at colleges. I passed a few bar exams as well. I always liked to do things and do them well regardless of my limitations.

Now that I'm achieving assurance in my new life, I feel my old self returning, with some changes. I've learned not to be as harsh on myself, and allow myself to make mistakes. I hope I've become modest, but who in the hell knows? All I know is that I'm smiling again.

CHAPTER THIRTEEN

THE GUILT CHALLENGE

When one goes blind, there are a lot of resources to help you learn how to adjust to the new life, but nobody tells how to deal with others' grief about your vision loss.

In the back of my mind, I realized that someday I would have to face total vision loss. People who cared for me would grieve for my loss.

And grief was something I never wanted.

The ironic thing is that many of my loved ones had a harder time adjusting to my blindness than I did. Not only did they have to watch me struggle to orient myself to the new world, but they had to change how they interacted with me. A lot of them felt a degree of guilt that I was the one going through this, while they had perfect sight.

This sentiment sets off a funny loop. They feel guilty about being spared of difficulties. I feel guilty that they feel guilty. They feel guilty about feeling guilty and making me feel guilty. And so on.

The guilt, by far, was the most difficult part of going blind. Logistics can be learned. Identity and self-perceptions can be adjusted. Guilt, is far more misleading, as it kept chipping away my relationship with my family and loved ones.

Change is hard, especially when it touches upon so many of the little things in life. I had to reconsider how I would read the mail? How would I write checks? How would I pay my bills? There were even unexpected questions like- What shoes should I wear when I walk everywhere? What should I do with my white cane when I have to carry bags?

At first, these questions are overwhelming and nobody has all of the answers. Afterall, the shift from partial sightedness into blindness is the hardest one. Hopefully, the changes after this one will be easier, since I'm getting better at being blind.

It is a life-changing event that can have a significant impact on our quality of life and daily activities.

The loss of vision eventually leads to a loss of independence, as we need assistance with daily activities that we once performed easily.

Additionally, blindness affects our emotional and psychological well-being. The loss of sight is a traumatic experience, and we experience anxiety and depression as we try to adjust to our new reality.

All and all, losing my sight was hard, but it was not unbearable.

I got used to my new lifeand learned how to do things differently.

We get just one life to live, so might just live!

For most of my life, it was relatively easy to adapt. I figure out ways to walk at night using memory and landmarks. I always walked behind people so I could tell that stairs were coming up based on their head movements. Once my determination was in place, It wasn't all that difficult to adjust to the small vision changes.

But there came a certain point, I lost enough vision that simple adaptions didn't cut it anymore and a desperate life shifting plan was required. It's a big lifestyle change.

I began navigating the world using a white cane, relying more on feel, sounds, patterns, and my remaining sight. I reorganized my house, and turned myself from an admitted snob into a reasonably tidy person.

I interacted with words in a new way through text to speech softwares on my computer.

I also had a passion for exploring the world. I loved to travel, hike, and experience new things. However, I was forced to adjust to a new way of living.

I loved the beauty of the world and the colors that surrounded me. But as my vision slowly faded, I began to focus on my other senses. I found that touch and smell were my new windows to the world.

I started to rely on my sense of touch to navigate my surroundings. I would run my fingers along the edges of walls and furniture, feeling my way around my home. I learned to identify different textures, from the smoothness of a glass surface to the roughness of a brick wall. With practice, I became more and more confident in my ability to navigate the world through touch alone.

I also began to rely on my sense of smell to help me experience the world around me. I found that certain scents could transport me to different places and times. The smell of freshly brewed coffee could take me to a cozy café, while the scent of pine trees could remind me of a trekking trail in the mountains.

With time, I learned to adapt to my vision loss and embrace my other senses. I found that the world was still full of beauty, even if I couldn't see it with my eyes. I continued to travel and explore, relying on touch and smell to guide me along the way.

On one particular adventure trip, I remember standing at the edge of the "cliff-jumping" point in Rishikesh, looking out at a stunning view of the river. I closed my eyes and took a deep breath, letting the fresh air fill my lungs. I reached out my hand and felt the rough texture of the rock beneath my fingers. In that moment, I realized that I didn't need my eyes to experience the beauty of the world. I had my other senses, and they were just as powerful.

Despite the challenges, many of us lead fulfilling and productive lives. There are numerous resources and support systems available to help us adapt to our new circumstances.

In conclusion, living with blindness can be a challenging and difficult journey. However, my willpower has helped me overcome these challenges and live a happy life. The ability to adapt and find ways to navigate the world without sight requires determination and strength.

Each one of us can achieve great success in all aspects of life, from personal relationships to professional careers. The journey may not always be fulfilling, but it is not impossible to live a satisfying life with blindness.

With the right support, resources, and mindset, we can continue to succeed and contribute to our society in meaningful ways.

CHAPTER FOURTEEN

SMART TECH MAKES BLIND SMARTER

My journey of adapting to new ways of life was and still is, challenging. But with the advancements in technology, it has become much easier. Smart devices have made it possible for blind individuals to perform tasks independently and live a more comfortable life.

One significant area where smart devices have made a difference is in household chores, such as cooking and washing. With the help of smart devices, a blind person can cook meals without assistance.

I use techniques and devices such as measuring cups with tactile markings and specialized cutting boards to safely prepare my food. Smart microwaves and cooktops have touchscreens that can read out cooking instructions and even adjust temperatures and cooking times automatically. Smart washing machines and talking dryers can also be controlled using voice commands, making laundry tasks more manageable. All you have to do is to hook them up with your smart phones through utility apps.

Talking smartphones have meaningfully upgraded the accessibility of blind users.

The voice assistants and built-in screen reader technology on smartphones, now allow us to navigate our phones, access information, and perform tasks without the need for sight.

For example, we can use voice commands to make calls, send texts, set location navigation, book cabs and do shopping. We can also use the screen reader to browse the internet, read emails, and access social media. In addition, many apps have built-in accessibility features, such as high contrast modes and speech-to-text functionality, making it easier for us to access information and interact with our phones.

Furthermore, talking smartphones have eliminated the need for specialized devices, such as scanners, braille note pads and tape recorders, which can be expensive and bulky to carry around. With a smartphone, we can have all the features we need in one device, which is compact and portable.

Case in point, talking smartphones have revolutionized the way blind individuals interact with technology, providing us with greater accessibility and independence in our daily lives.

Smart devices have also made entertainment more accessible to blind individuals. Audio books and podcasts can be accessed through smart speakers and smart phones on tap of a button.

Streaming services like Netflix and Amazon Prime offer audio descriptions for many of their shows and movies. These are regular movies which have an additional audio track that provides descriptive narration of the visual elements on screen for the benefit of viewers who are blind or visually impaired.

Audio description is a technology that allows us to better understand and enjoy the movie by telling us of what is happening on screen.

Pre-recorded voice of a person, in form of audio narration is played during pauses in dialogue, and it describes the important visual elements of the scene, such as the characters' expressions, body language, and movements, as well as the location, action, and other key details that are not conveyed through dialogues.

In addition to this, I also use smart home devices like Amazon Echo and Apple HomePod to control everything from the lights to the indoor temperature with specific voice commands.

I have also programmed my smart home devices to notify me of important events, appointments and shopping reminders.

It's important to remember that taking control of our life involves more than just using technology, though. It's about setting goals, making a plan, and taking action to achieve those goals also. By incorporating smart devices into my routine, I'm using tools to help me achieve my goals more efficiently and effectively.

However, it's important to note here that not all blind people have access to or can afford this technology, so efforts should be made by every blind individual to work hard and make themselves financially worthy of these advancements.

Overall, smart technology can provide us with new opportunities for communication, learning, and independence, which can help us to become more knowledgeable and empowered individuals.